Spoken Word of a Cooks

Jose Nerie M. Roca

BookLeaf
Publishing

India | USA | UK

Presentation by *BookLeaf Publishing*

Web: www.bookleafpub.com

E-mail: info@bookleafpub.com

ISBN : 9789357447096

First edition 2021

DEDICATION

I dedicate it to God Almighty, my self, my love , my friends, my colleges and to my family.

And to those Aspiring individuals who are in the verge of giving up but they choose to fight. May your never-ending fighting spirit guide you to your success.

ACKNOWLEDGEMENT

I would like to express my special thanks to my friends and colleges for giving an opportunity to learn and to feel the support when I need it the most. To those people who see my talents and to those people that push me up. To my family who I loved where they never stop on supporting me. May we all be blessed by God everyday of our life.

PREFACE

This book tackles life, Love, Passion and career in a form of poems that may motivate those aspiring cooks and chefs around the world. It may be funny but kitchen life is tough that only the strongest people can survive. This book may give you idea on how cooks and chefs feel when they are alone base on experience.

Life

Love is what we are made of.
Individually we are seeking love
For we are made to socialize
Even we are alone today.

Life is a blessing made by God
Intellectually designed
For us to go forward
Each time we fell short.

Leave those worries away,
In time you may succeed
For you are great
End is the word for those who never believe to
their self.

Love

Loosing is hard if you focus on it
Over time you may be destroyed
Value it so you may learn
Ending is not an option.

Leave those things that may stressed you,
Overthinking may harm you.
Verily love is a gift that may empower you to
succeed.
Each failure may give you a chance to assess
your life.

Look forward my friend for you are made to
succeed.
Old ways may be good but changes is better.
Victory is on your hands.
Elevate your self from the failures to make it
better.

Passion

Playing is the word we may forget when we
grow older,
Action can be tiering as we grow older
Self is a word that we never value
Sort it out so you may understand
In pain we grow in time we may heal.
Offer your self time so it may glow.
Never give up so you may succeed in the path
that you choose.

Career

Careful on things that you will choose in life
Action is the word that may help you to start
Rare things can be found for those who never stop
Error is part of growth.
Each time you worry, can consume your opportunities.
Road in career is tough, but be passionate so you may succeed.

Knife Skills

Dreaming is facile,
But making it work is hard.
Dreaming to be a CHEF is facile,
But achieving it is hard.
Cooking is facile they verbally express,
But doing it is hard.
Life is hard I verbally express,
But living is facile.

Knife adeptness is facile they verbalize,
But congruous technique is needed.
Learning to slice and chop is like learning how
to live.
First you required to ken what kind of knife you
require,
just like what kind of partner I require.
Second is learning to jullienne, dice, and
chipponade,
is like learning how to interact
Third is sharpening and honing your knife is
consequential,
just like reading and integrating cognizance to
your self.

Lastly learn to be cautious because Knife is like
a life that will cut you and make you bleed until
you give up.

Kitchen

Shit happens everyday, where you cant do
anything on it.
Kitchen is a place where you don't want to be.
A place where everything is contaminated of
different substances.
A place where dreamers are shattered in to
pieces.
A place where your whole life is consume like a
candle.
A place where forgotten people of society today
find a family.
A place where egoistic, dreamer, confused and a
believer understand each other.
A place where you will suffer in different kind
of anxiety.
A place where there is no room for a selfish
personality.
A place where demons becomes angels.
A place where easy life become uneasy.
But before you think twice my friend, just clear
your thoughts.
Because by the end of the day the most caring
and the most humble persons are in the kitchen.
At the end of the day enjoy and celebrate it
because you made your self a favor.

At the end of the day your team made a good
service where everyone is smiling.

Recipe

One half, one forth, and three forth
what kind of numbers are they?
I realized that a recipe is like making a plan for
your life.
At first you have to I identify what dish you
wanna make.
Then it is a Goal.
Second is to gather all the right ingredients for
your recipe.
Then it is looking for right friends and partner in
life.
Third is looking for a right equipment.
Then it is looking for a right knowledge and
skills.
Fourth is to find the right weight of every
ingredients.
Then it is making a right decision in life.
Fifth is the to put the proper procedure in your
recipe.
Then it is when you start to get experience and
learning from your mistakes.
And finally you cook and serve your dish.
Then this is the fruit of your labors after you
reach your goals.

Cooking

Chowder, filet mignon and steak
Those are fancy food we serve on the kitchen,
To feed those pretentious people who only look
for there own.
How we cook is the way how we express our
emotions.
Slicing and chopping ingredients is the the part
of our career.
Sautéing is the start of our greatness.
but before we end up of doing what we like, Mis
en place is our key to our success.
Lots of cooks claim different kinds of secret
ingredients.
But the real secret ingredients is the
determination and love for our craft.
And never forget where we learn how to cook,
it's a gift from our mom who always nourish us.

Mise en Place

Simple things we always put aside.
as if we don't think it's important in the kitchen.
and I thought it was important in life too.
Such as experienced chefs, that their lives
revolve around the job they choose.
As someone who dreams and loves, sometimes
we forget the importance of harmony and setting
aside the word readiness.
But while I am gaining experience in that
profession of my choice.
I thought it was important to be prepared as
well.
In the things I will deal with.
In things I don't have to miss.
In things that are only small if you look at them.
Preparing and putting things in the right place is
important, just as you deal with the world of
uncertainty.
So to my friends and dreamers, mise en place is
an important teaching of the chefs that you can
not only apply in the kitchen but also in your
life.

We Bake

We are all afraid of things that are always
calculated.
Such as the elementary seemingly terrified of the
question of mathematics.
Baking a loaf is like the life of a normal person.
The first part is to combine essential ingredients
such as yeast, flour and water. Yeast is like our
brain that gives us lift.
Flour is like our body that gives weight and
value.
and water is like glue that gives us the
opportunity to make our dreams come true.
And the hands of the baker will be the shapers of
our lives,
and the heat of the oven will be the world that
will give us the opportunity to stand the test.
and the last part is up to us to choose the right
time.
Baking is not a simple thing like our lives that
must be measured and monitored.

Sauté

Cooking begins with sautéing the ingredients in
a hot pan and slowly adding spices to give the
food a unique kick.
And I will mix it with love that only I know how
to give.
With every gesture of my hands and with the
slow opening of my lips, utters the words that I
cannot say to the person I adore.
And as the soup thickens, I will also put the
ingredients that need to be softened along with
my heart which is also slowly thickening with its
soft words. and gives hope to my hopeful heart.

As we approach the last part of cooking, the
smells appear that seem to invite you to adore
me too.
And before I put out the fire of my stove,
 I will first taste and observe what is missing.
Is it pepper or salt that is missing? or is it too
salty? that you occasionally avoid my sight? or
lack of salt? so that you will notice me?
or is it lacking in pepper? which will give a little
sharpness to my speech to arouse your eyes.
My dear, here is my dish that has been prepared
and not neglected so that with every bite you

make you may also feel that you are important to
me.

Uniform

Uniforms give us respect and dignity as cooks.
Uniforms also provide protection against
dangerous objects in the kitchen.
But the most important thing is that the uniform
gives us good discipline. Discipline that can be
brought and will remind us to be prepared for all
trials.
we need to respect the uniform we have.
If you want to be proficient in the profession that
you choose you need to organize, respect and
take care of it.

Support

Cold and hot inside the kitchen.
Ohh dear I'm going to work again,
I'll start cooking again for our future.
As we look forward to a better future, I will try
to work every day to fulfill our desires.
My dear, I'm sorry for being too late on my way
home.
My dear, I'm sorry if I don't have time to say
hello to you.
For by the time of my arrival I was already
exhausted.
My dear, let you and I recover from my
shortcomings as long as you always believe in
me, and I will make the day happy to be with
you.

My dear, all our hardships and efforts will bear
fruit as well.
Thank you so much for your tireless support and
understanding.

Taste

Grade 4 when I started dreaming of cooking.
Because of my dear mother, I started holding a knife to cut vegetables.
And on every day that God made, dear mother always wakes up early to cook breakfast.
I will never forget the taste of the dishes he served at our table.
Only memories of her cooking I remembered fragrant dishes I seemed to taste at the tip of my tongue.
My dear mother forgive me for the times I am far away to reach my dreams, Hope that I will not disappoint you in every decision I make towards my dream.
In the future you will celebrate my success and re-taste the dishes that shaped my dreams.
To my dear mother, father, brothers and sisters, expect me to come home again so that we can complete our dinner table again.

Leadership

It's hard to start in the kitchen without knowing how to adapt to new chefs.
And it's even harder to get in and work in the kitchen if they find out you're from culinary school, they'll test how much you know and what you can do. you will be laughed at for wasting money on cooking.
But what they don't know is that it's not just cooking.
Here you will learn how to get along, make friends, think and understand.
Understand the distrust of people.
Here you can also understand that people will believe you and trust you if you can show them that you know what you are doing.
So here comes your leadership that you can't fully understand just outside of university studies.
Education will give you greater understanding to guide those who are proud and those who despise you.
My friends always remember that respect is priceless.
Respect is reaped by showing the respect that you know is right.

Culture

Culture is essential for man to move forward.
And in every place there is a new culture to
develop.
Culture that will give life to the modern
generation.
which if you review is refreshing.
In every kitchen there is a culture you can't
change.
The culture of brotherhood and appreciation for
the food they love and the country they came
from.

Soul

Cooking is endless and without judgment.
only a love of cooking can reconcile each race.
Only food can calm two people arguing.
Food can also cause them to argue.
But as a cook our job is to unite people who
argue, love each other and believer that there is
peace in heaven.

Constructive Criticism

With every shout and criticism you will receive.
With every sweat and blood you offer towards your dream.
Do not lose courage and determination.
Every time you wake up early and when you go to sleep late don't forget to thank our dear God, because of every hardship and sorrow He will not leave you.
Do not be discouraged, because in the kitchen there is always hope for the industrious and persevering person.

Heart and Soul

Put away your fears
Strengthen your mind
Save your heart.
Taste the hardship
Accept your weakness.
this is what will bring you success

Believe in him

Believe in yourself that every effort you make has a reward
Believe in yourself you will prosper.
Believe in yourself not everyone can trust you.
Believe in yourself you can resist all who despise you.
Believe in yourself that you are the only way for you to reach your dream.
With every sweat you offer yourself, there is hope to come to you.
Think that you are not alone because even if you believe in yourself only God will give you the strength to fight.
Pray for guidance and protection from any disaster.

Never forget

don't forget to smile and be happy with the little things.
don't forget to fall in love again.
don't forget someone believes in you.
don't forget there are good people still coming to you.
don't forget your dreams.
don't forget your parents.
don't forget your best friends.
never forget that there is a God who guides you.
don't forget to smile and be happy with the little things.
don't forget to fall in love again.
don't forget someone believes in you.
don't forget there are good people still coming to you.
don't forget your dreams.
don't forget your parents.
don't forget your best friends.
never forget that there is a god who guides you.
There will be no great person that has never experience to taste the rock bottom of life.
Be grateful because you are on the right path.